INSIDE!

YOUR AWESOME MATCH ANNUAL 2014!

10636875

ANNUAL 2014

INSIDE! ≫ World's 50 Greatest Goalscorers ≫ Crazy Facts ≫ Funny Pics ≫ Quizzes ≫ Next Big Thing & more!

MEGA VALUE! THE ONLY FOOTY ANNUAL WORTH BUYING!

GOAL MACHINES 18

BRAZIL 2014 69

RICHEST STARS 64

BALE REVEALED 56

NEXT BIG THING 50

STARS' CARS 80

SUBSCRIBE TO MATCH – TURN TO PAGE 92 FOR MORE INFO!

NEYMAR!
WILL 2014 BE HIS YEAR?

The Brazil wonderkid is ready to become a world superstar!

Neymar is gunning for the World Cup, Champions League, La Liga and loads more big trophies in his quest to become the world's best player! MATCH takes a closer look at why 2014 could be his year!

WORLD CUP!

All eyes will be on Brazil next summer as they host the biggest competition in footy - the World Cup! Neymar will be under massive pressure to deliver in front of nearly 200 million Brazilians, and we reckon he could own the tournament!

BARCELONA!

The Spanish giants are desperate to become the best club team on the planet again - and new signing Neymar could help them do it! His link-up play with Lionel Messi, Andres Iniesta and Xavi totally owns defenders all across Europe!

Neymar became Barcelona's second most expensive star ever when he joined for £48.6 million back in May!

AWESOME TRICKS!

Neymar doesn't just score jaw-dropping goals! MATCH readers love him because he tries flash stepovers, rabonas and loads more mind-blowing tricks in every game! We need to see more stars do that!

BALE hits the big time!

GARETH BALE's red-hot form in 2013 turned him into a star and sealed his move to Madrid!

BALE'S FOOTY'S NO.1 STAR, MATCH!

TV KING!

BT Sport hired Bale to help promote their new channel, while he also starred in an advert in New York for Premier League coverage in the USA!

I LOVE BEING ON THE BOX!

THE REAL DEAL!

After months of speculation, Spanish giants Real Madrid signed Bale for £85.3 million on September 1! He agreed a six-year deal and instantly became one of the world's best-paid sportsmen!

AND WE'LL STAY UP, TOO!

DID YOU KNOW?

Cardiff became the 46th club to play in the Premier League when they battled West Ham back in August!

FALCAO'S LOADED!

I'VE GOT FIVE FERRARIS, TOO!

Colombia striker Radamel Falcao earns a wallet-busting £15.7 million a year at Monaco! That works out at 50p a second! Lend us a tenner, mate!

COVER STAR!

After scoring loads of wicked goals and winning awards for fun, EA Sports put Bale on the FIFA 14 cover with Messi! The Wales ace was motion captured for the game, too!

IT'S A BIT WARM IN THIS!

PLAYER OF THE YEAR!

The Wales superhero became only the fifth star in history to win the famous PFA Player Of The Year award TWICE! Bale bagged the Young Player Of The Year award, too!

WE NEED A BIGGER TROPHY CABINET!

CELEBRITY FANS!

Check out which clubs these massive stars support!

DANIEL CRAIG
Liverpool

ANDY MURRAY
Arsenal

USAIN BOLT
Man. United

WILL FERRELL
Chelsea

RUSSELL BRAND
West Ham

GERARD BUTLER
Celtic

LEBRON JAMES
Liverpool

RAFAEL NADAL
Real Madrid

BENTEKE'S SPACE FANS!

CHRISTIAN BENTEKE is so good, fans come to see him from all over the universe!

BENTEKE IS OUT OF THIS WORLD

MY CAT'S CALLED RON!

AWKWARD!

Real Madrid star Isco has a dog called Messi! Cristiano Ronaldo won't give him treats if he comes to The Bernabeu!

MESSI
THE £215 MILLION MAN!

£215 MILLION IS A TOTAL BARGAIN!

Mega-rich **PSG** are ready to offer **Barça** £215 million for **Lionel Messi**! MATCH takes a look at what the French giants could buy instead of the world's greatest player!

PSG COULD BUY...
616,045 PS4 consoles!

PSG COULD BUY...

Cristiano Ronaldo (£80 million)

+

Radamel Falcao (£51 million)

+

Neymar (£49 million)

+

Stevan Jovetic (£22 million)

+

Iago Aspas (£7 million)

+

Arouna Kone (£6 million)

PSG COULD BUY...
13.5 million copies of Wreck-It Ralph on DVD!

DO NOT PASS GO!

Striker Darren Bent told MATCH he loves playing Monopoly! Benty said, "When I'm playing with my family, it can get pretty heated!"

MONOPOLY
BELFAST EDITION

YOU OWE ME MONEY, AGAIN!

CRAZY FACES!

Check out this mad Uruguay fan! We have no idea how he saw the game!

I'M TOTALLY QUACKERS MATCH!

YEP, I'VE WON THIS THREE TIMES!

IS MESSI WORTH IT?

✓ He's won six La Liga titles, two Copa del Rey trophies and three Champions Leagues! Not bad!

✓ Messi scored 96 La Liga goals in 2011-12 and 2012-13 combined! It sounds like a joke, but it's not!

✓ He dribbles past defenders for fun, breaks tons of records and sells more shirts than Topman!

VERDICT: YES, HE'S WORTH £215 MILLION!

WORLD CUP STAT ATTACK!

Check out all the coolest World Cup stats ahead of this summer's big kick-off!

5 Brazil have won the most World Cup trophies with five, including their last one back in 2002!

171 171 goals were scored at the 1998 World Cup in France - that's a record! Hopefully it'll be broken in Brazil this summer!

4 Germany have lost in four World Cup finals, including 1966 when England beat them 4-2!

15 Brazil legend Ronaldo has scored the most goals in World Cup history with a net-busting 15 strikes!

1 Spain won all four knockout games 1-0 at the 2010 World Cup, including the final against Holland!

25 Germany legend Lothar Matthaus has played the most World Cup games - 25 between 1982 and 1998!

3 Brazil legend Cafu has played in a record three World Cup finals, winning two and losing one!

Zlatan's ON FIRE!

EVEN MY GUFFS ARE RED HOT!

IBRAHIMOVIĆ 10

That's how good PSG goal machine Zlatan Ibrahimovic was in 2013!

PARIS SAINT-GERMAIN 1970

FERGIE'S TROPHIES!

Sir Alex Ferguson won the Prem title in 13 of the 21 seasons before he retired! What a legend!

MANCHESTER UNITED

1

ROCKING ROBIN!

Man. United superstar Robin van Persie owned 2013, but we reckon he'll be even better in 2014! His close control, first touch, footy brain, tricks and lethal left foot can turn any game!

2

WICKED WORLD CUP!

There will be loads of quality footy in 2014, but nothing can beat the thrill and drama of the World Cup! It only comes around once every four years, so get ready for football fireworks!

3

LIVERPOOL'S NEW STAR!

The Reds are desperate to hit the big time again and tricky Brazil star Philippe Coutinho could be the man to get them in the Champo League! The midfielder's rapid pace, dribbling, eye for goal and passing are out of this world!

5 REASONS WHY....
2014 WILL ROCK!

MATCH checks out why 2014 is going to be an awesome year of footy!

5

SUPER JACK IS BACK!

2014 could be huge for Jack Wilshere! England fans are expecting him to become their new superstar and Arsenal are ready to build their whole team around him! He totally rocks!

4

TITLE RACE!

Man. United blew everyone away last season, but they'll face a bigger battle for the Premier League title in 2014! The Manchester derby on March 1 will be epic, and Chelsea will fight until the end!

The red-hot Poland striker scored an incredible 23 goals in just 21 games for club and country between December 16 and April 20 last season!

Lewa became the first player ever to score four goals in a Champions League semi-final when he ripped Real Madrid to pieces in April!

The awesome goal king married Polish karate champion Anna Stachurska on June 22 at a massive event in Warsaw!

LEWANDOWSKI

SNAPPED!

BEST OF 2013 SPECIAL!

PART ONE!

STAY COOL, LADS!

I'LL JUST SAY I'M FAT!

LET'S GET THE CORNER FLAGS, TOO!

Utrecht must be skint if they're nicking footballs!

DON'T LET PUYOL CHANGE MY NAPPY!

Messi has been acting like a real dummy lately!

Heitinga loves busting out his deadly crocodile tackle! Ouch!

SNAP ATTACK!

I WANTED BURGER KING!

Cisse's not happy when he finds out it's KFC for tea!

DAVID'S AFRO IS MUCH WORSE!

ONE LUIZ IS ENOUGH, THANKS!

Neymar and Thiago Silva aren't impressed with Dani Alves' rubbish impression of Brazil team-mate David Luiz!

I NEED SOME NEW SHORTS!

It looks like Bale couldn't hold out until half-time to use the loo!

MOO-VE OUTTA MY WAY!

Routledge shows Chico why he's got no future in bull fighting!

IT'S SNOW JOKE!

Guzan will never go sledging without his sledge again!

WOW, IT'S SO LIGHT!

I'M PLAYING CANDY CRUSH!

Walcott and Podolski test the new invisible iPad!

CRAZY HAIR

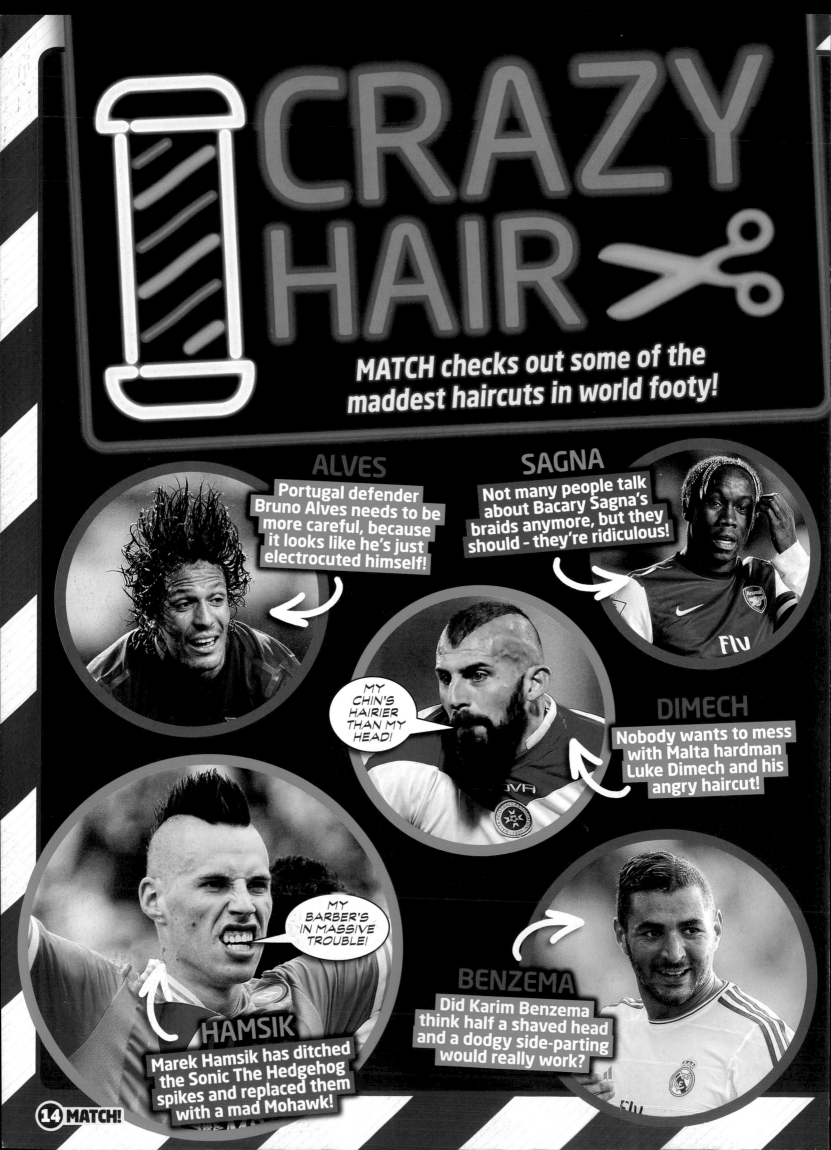

MATCH checks out some of the maddest haircuts in world footy!

ALVES

Portugal defender Bruno Alves needs to be more careful, because it looks like he's just electrocuted himself!

SAGNA

Not many people talk about Bacary Sagna's braids anymore, but they should – they're ridiculous!

MY CHIN'S HAIRIER THAN MY HEAD!

DIMECH

Nobody wants to mess with Malta hardman Luke Dimech and his angry haircut!

MY BARBER'S IN MASSIVE TROUBLE!

HAMSIK

Marek Hamsik has ditched the Sonic The Hedgehog spikes and replaced them with a mad Mohawk!

BENZEMA

Did Karim Benzema think half a shaved head and a dodgy side-parting would really work?

Premier League BRAIN-BUSTER!

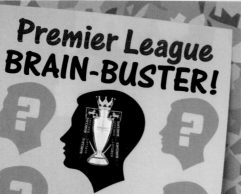

How much do you know about the Prem?

1. Which team did Arsenal score more Prem goals against last season – Newcastle, West Ham or Reading?

2. How many goal machines bagged over 20 Premier League strikes in 2012-13?

3. Man. United, Man. City, Chelsea, Arsenal and which other team have won the Premier League title?

4. Can you name the Premier League's all-time leading goalscorer?

5. How many clubs have played in the Premier League since its first season in 1992-93 – 36, 46 or 56?

6. Who is the oldest ever outfield Premier League player – Ryan Giggs, Teddy Sheringham or Paul Scholes?

7. Who are this season's Premier League sponsors – Barclays, Pepsi, EA Sports or Coca-Cola?

8. How many games does each team play during a single Premier League season – 34, 38 or 42?

9. Who grabbed the most assists in the Prem last season – Juan Mata, Santi Cazorla or Steven Gerrard?

10. Which 2013-14 Premier League team are nicknamed The Bluebirds?

1 ....
2 ....
3 ....
4 ....
5 ....
6 ....
7 ....
8 ....
9 ....
10 ....

ANSWERS ON PAGE 90

RVP bagged against Fulham on his first start for United last season, and hit a match-winning hat-trick in the next game against Southampton!

Van Persie scored an incredible 30 goals for The Red Devils in all competitions and six for the Holland national team in 2012-13! Hero!

He was named United's Fans' Player Of The Year, made the Prem Team Of The Year and picked up the Prem Golden Boot and his first league title!

VAN PERSIE

THE WORLD'S 50 GREATEST GOALSCORERS!

MATCH counts down the Top 50 greatest goal machines on the planet right now!

FRED

50

Club: *Fluminense*
Country: *Brazil*

Fred hasn't made a massive impact at club level, but he's been busting nets for fun in international footy! The Brazil striker's deadly double in the Confederations Cup final against Spain last summer was quality!

PIERRE-EMERICK AUBAMEYANG

48

Club: *Borussia Dortmund*
Country: *Gabon*

The Gabon wonderkid ripped up Ligue 1 for the last two seasons at Saint-Etienne, bagged a huge £13 million move to Dortmund, then scored a stunning hat-trick on his Bundesliga debut! He's gonna be a world superstar!

BOOTS

NIKE HYPERVENOM

FERNANDO TORRES

47

Club: *Chelsea*
Country: *Spain*

El Nino gets loads of stick, but on his day he's still a world-class finisher! He's scored in the last two European Championship finals for Spain, and also netted a quality goal in the 2013 Europa League Final! Legend!

ARJEN ROBBEN

49

Club: *Bayern Munich*
Country: *Holland*

The Bayern Munich superstar has always been famous for his electric pace, deadly dribbling and assists, but his shooting has improved big-time! His ice-cool finish in the Champions League final last May proved his class!

DID YOU KNOW?

ROBBEN HAS WON THE PREMIER LEAGUE, EREDIVISIE, LA LIGA AND BUNDESLIGA TITLES!

DIMITAR BERBATOV

46

Club: *Fulham*
Country: *Bulgaria*

We love watching Berba play! He's ice-cool in front of goal, has one of the best footy brains around and tries shots no other striker would! Nobody in world football scores better goals than him with the outside of the boot!

BOOTS

ADIDAS PREDATOR LZ

OLIVIER GIROUD

BOOTS
PUMA
PUMA EVOSPEED

45

Club: *Arsenal*
Country: *France*

Giroud is a lethal goal machine and he'll only get better, because he can finish in so many ways! He leaps in the air like an NBA basketball superstar, loves bullet headers and has a left foot like a rocket launcher! He's class!

THEO WALCOTT

44

Club: *Arsenal*
Country: *England*

Theo has been called the Usain Bolt of football because of his electric speed, but he proved he was more than just pace in 2012-13 with 14 Prem goals! His one-on-one finishing is up there with the world's best!

PAPISS CISSE

DID YOU KNOW?

CISSE WON THE PREM GOAL OF THE SEASON AWARD IN 2011-12, JUST FOUR MONTHS AFTER JOINING NEWCASTLE!

42

Club: *Newcastle*
Country: *Senegal*

The Senegal goal machine is the king of St. James' Park! Magpies fans love net-busting strikers and Cisse is a crowd favourite! His movement makes defenders look silly, and he can bust the net from anywhere on the pitch!

WILFRIED BONY

43

Club: *Swansea*
Country: *Ivory Coast*

The lethal Ivory Coast superstar slammed home 31 Eredivisie goals for Vitesse Arnhem last season before bagging a club record £12 million move to The Swans! His power and finishing give defenders nightmares!

HENRIKH MKHITARYAN

41

Club: *Borussia Dortmund*
Country: *Armenia*

Mkhitaryan is probably Armenia's greatest player of all time! The attacking midfielder burst onto the footy stage last season with Shakhtar Donetsk, and his class finishing skills bagged him a big summer move to Dortmund!

STEVAN JOVETIC

40

Club: Man. City
Country: Montenegro

The Montenegro trickster has always been famous for his silky dribbling and clever turns, but his shooting skills improved big time in 2013! His £22 million fee could be a bargain for City – especially if he fires them to the Prem title!

DEMBA BA

39

Club: Chelsea
Country: Senegal

Ba only started 19 Prem games for Newcastle last season before moving to Stamford Bridge, but he still finished 2012-13 as The Magpies' top scorer – he's lethal! He could be a game-changing super sub for Chelsea in 2014!

DID YOU KNOW?

DEFOE IS ONE OF ONLY FOUR STARS IN PREM HISTORY TO SCORE FIVE GOALS IN ONE GAME!

JERMAIN DEFOE

38

Club: Tottenham
Country: England

Defoe has been hurt by Roberto Soldado's arrival at White Hart Lane, but he's still one of the best finishers on the planet! He only needs half a yard of space to squeeze a shot past defenders and into the net!

OSCAR CARDOZO

37

Club: Benfica
Country: Paraguay

The lanky Paraguay striker has been around for ages, but he's still busting nets every week! He helped Portuguese giants Benfica reach the 2013 Europa League Final with seven goals in seven starts in the tournament!

SAMUEL ETO'O

36

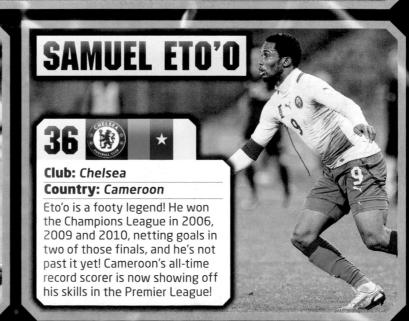

Club: Chelsea
Country: Cameroon

Eto'o is a footy legend! He won the Champions League in 2006, 2009 and 2010, netting goals in two of those finals, and he's not past it yet! Cameroon's all-time record scorer is now showing off his skills in the Premier League!

MARIO GOMEZ

35

Club: *Fiorentina*
Country: *Germany*

German giants Bayern Munich might regret selling Mario Gomez to Fiorentina, because he's still got bags of goals in him! His movement in the box confuses centre-backs and he pounces on chances like a predator!

FRANK LAMPARD

33

Club: *Chelsea*
Country: *England*

Lamps is the king of sniffing out goals from midfield! He loves sneaking into the 18-yard box and punishing opponents with his clever movement and lethal finishing, and he's got one of the best long shots in the world!

DANIEL STURRIDGE

32

Club: *Liverpool*
Country: *England*

Sturridge's nickname should be Optimus Prime, because he 'transformed' himself from a bench warmer into a red-hot goal machine in 2013! He's still got tons of pace and tricks, but now he can finish like a king!

DIDIER DROGBA

34

Club: *Galatasaray*
Country: *Ivory Coast*

Drog is a real football legend! The Ivory Coast powerhouse tore holes in nets with his rocket shots and bullet headers for Chelsea between 2004 and 2012, and now he's doing it for Turkish champions Galatasaray!

MICHU

DID YOU KNOW?

MICHU BAGGED FOUR GOALS IN HIS FIRST THREE PREMIER LEAGUE GAMES FOR THE SWANS!

31

Club: *Swansea*
Country: *Spain*

Swansea's £2 million deal to sign Michu from Rayo Vallecano in 2012 might go down in history as one of the biggest Premier League bargains ever! His left foot is like a magic wand and goalkeepers can't handle it!

MARIO MANDZUKIC

30 FC BAYERN MÜNCHEN

Club: *Bayern Munich*
Country: *Croatia*

Mandzukic was a pretty average striker until Euro 2012, but after a great tournament with Croatia and a treble-winning season with Bayern Munich in 2012-13, he's become a world superstar! Could 2014 be even better?

DID YOU KNOW?
MANDZUKIC IS THE ONLY CROATIA PLAYER IN HISTORY TO SCORE IN A CHAMPIONS LEAGUE FINAL!

MARIO BALOTELLI

27 AC MILAN

Club: *AC Milan*
Country: *Italy*

Balotelli started showing his true potential in 2013 after joining Milan from Man. City and scoring almost every week! He's the best penalty taker on the planet, loves long shots and has improved his work-rate big time in Italy!

ROMELU LUKAKU

BOOTS
NIKE MERCURIAL VAPOR IX

29 Everton

Club: *Everton*
Country: *Belgium*

Romelu Lukaku will become one of the world's top five strikers in the next few years, because he's still learning his game! The Belgium beast has got the pace, passion, strength and shooting power to be a global superstar!

STEFAN KIESSLING

28 Bayer Leverkusen

Club: *Bayer Leverkusen*
Country: *Germany*

Only one man scored more Bundesliga goals than Robert Lewandowski last season, and that was Leverkusen's Stefan Kiessling! The lanky striker is a fox in the box and loves busting nets with powerful headers!

BURAK YILMAZ

26 Galatasaray Turkey

Club: *Galatasaray*
Country: *Turkey*

Yilmaz has blasted onto the world stage after an incredible year with Galatasaray! He was top scorer in the Turkish Super Lig with 24 goals and netted eight strikes in the Champions League. His finishing is lethal!

ALVARO NEGREDO

25

Club: Man. City
Country: Spain

Negredo scored 25 goals in just 34 La Liga starts for Sevilla last season, and now he's ready to blast Man. City to Prem glory! He outmuscles defenders like a WWE wrestler and is one of Europe's best strikers in the air!

CARLOS TEVEZ

24

Club: Juventus
Country: Argentina

Italian champions Juventus must be laughing about signing Tevez for just £12 million last summer! The 29-year-old runs his socks off for the team, but has real quality too! His one-on-one skills, volleys and free-kicks are class!

STEPHAN EL SHAARAWY

DID YOU KNOW?

EL SHAARAWY HAS BEEN COMPARED TO CRISTIANO RONALDO FOR HIS LETHAL PACE AND DRIBBLING SKILLS!

23

Club: AC Milan
Country: Italy

El Shaarawy has got more than just a crazy Mohawk haircut! The Pharaoh mixes confidence and lethal finishing skills with rapid acceleration to make the ultimate striker! He'll be Milan and Italy's main man very soon!

CHRISTIAN BENTEKE

22

Club: Aston Villa
Country: Belgium

Benteke became world famous in 2013 after an incredible debut season in the Prem! The Villa goal machine's bone-crushing power, shooting and scary heading skills make him a defender's worst nightmare!

ROBERTO SOLDADO

21

Club: Tottenham
Country: Spain

Spurs smashed their transfer record to sign Roberto Soldado for £26 million back in August – that's how good he is! His expert finishing and magic movement helped him net 24 La Liga goals for Valencia last season!

JACKSON MARTINEZ

20

Club: *Porto*
Country: *Colombia*

The Colombia hitman has been one of the breakthrough stars of 2013! He won the top scorer award in Portugal's Primeira Liga after netting 26 goals in his debut season – six more than closest rival Lima! He's lethal!

EDIN DZEKO

19

Club: *Man. City*
Country: *Bosnia*

We reckon Dzeko is one of the most underrated stars in world footy! He spends more time on the bench than a weightlifter but his movement, footy brain and finishing destroys defenders whenever he's on the pitch!

BOOTS
ADIDAS PREDATOR LZ

KLAAS-JAN HUNTELAAR

18

Club: *Schalke*
Country: *Holland*

It's almost impossible to stop The Hunter when he brings his A-game onto the pitch! His clever movement baffles centre-backs, his right foot is like a rocket and his heading accuracy is unreal! MATCH loves watching him play!

WAYNE ROONEY

DID YOU KNOW?
WAZZA WAS NAMED ENGLAND PLAYER OF THE YEAR IN 2008 AND 2009!

16

Club: *Man. United*
Country: *England*

Wazza is mega passionate and is still one of the best net-busters in world footy! When the England striker's on top form, he barges past defenders like the Incredible Hulk and blasts thunderous shots through nets like a cannonball!

KARIM BENZEMA

17

Club: *Real Madrid*
Country: *France*

Benzema has been in Cristiano Ronaldo's shadow for years at The Bernabeu, but he's still one of Europe's deadliest goal kings! Keepers hate it when he goes through on goal, because he finishes like a total machine!

MARCO REUS

15 BVB 09

Club: *Borussia Dortmund*
Country: *Germany*

'Rolls Reus' has become one of Europe's hottest stars over the last two years, and he'll get even better in 2014! He's got the speed of a leopard, magic dribbling and inch-perfect finishing skills! He's going to be a footy legend!

GARETH BALE

13

Club: *Real Madrid*
Country: *Wales*

Bale has always been famous for blistering pace, expert crossing and raw power but his free-kicks, one-on-one finishing and rocket shots helped him to legendary status in 2013! The Wales hero scores goals from anywhere!

BOOTS

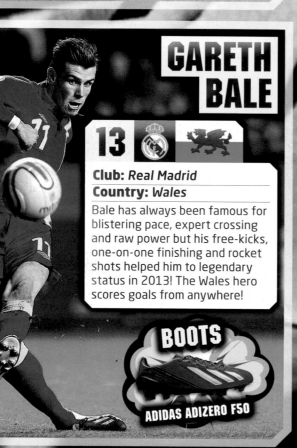

ADIDAS ADIZERO F50

ANTONIO DI NATALE

12

Club: *Udinese*
Country: *Italy*

Di Natale is absolutely ancient, but he's still smashing nets every week in Italy! He's hit 23 league goals or more in each of the last four Serie A seasons, which is crazy! We reckon he'll still be scoring goals when he's 90!

THOMAS MULLER

14 FC BAYERN MÜNCHEN

Club: *Bayern Munich*
Country: *Germany*

There's no forward in world footy who sniffs out space and scoring chances like Thomas Muller! His movement and intelligence helped him net three goals against Barcelona in the 2013 Champions League Semi-Final!

GONZALO HIGUAIN

DID YOU KNOW?

GONZO WAS BORN IN FRANCE, BUT CHOSE TO PLAY INTERNATIONAL FOOTY FOR ARGENTINA LIKE HIS DAD!

11 N

Club: *Napoli*
Country: *Argentina*

Arsenal nearly bought Higuain from Real Madrid last summer, but Napoli grabbed him at the last minute for £34.5 million! The Serie A giants are laughing now, because the Argentina ace's movement and finishing rule!

NEYMAR

DID YOU KNOW?
NEYMAR WON THE GOLDEN BALL FOR BEING THE BEST PLAYER AT LAST SUMMER'S CONFEDS CUP!

10

Club: *Barcelona*
Country: *Brazil*

MATCH can't get enough of the Brazil wonderkid's jaw-dropping flicks and tricks! Simon Cowell thinks Britain's Got Talent but we reckon Neymar's Got Talent, because his flash skills make defenders look like total fools!

SERGIO AGUERO

9

Club: *Man. City*
Country: *Argentina*

Man. City's record signing is the ultimate striker package! He mixes deadly finishing skills with rapid acceleration to make a devastating goal king! Can Kun repeat his 2011-12 Prem title-winning heroics in 2014?

EDINSON CAVANI

BOOTS
ADIDAS ADIZERO F50

8

Club: *PSG*
Country: *Uruguay*

PSG paid Napoli a mind-blowing £55 million for Cavani in July, and he's worth every single penny! The Uruguay bulldozer bagged 29 goals in 33 Serie A starts last season, before bringing his lethal shooting skills to France!

ZLATAN IBRAHIMOVIC

7

Club: *PSG*
Country: *Sweden*

Zlatan is a total beast! He hit 30 Ligue 1 goals for PSG last season, which was 11 more than his closest rival - how crazy is that? His confidence is through the roof, but he backs it up by playing footy like a legend!

LUIS SUAREZ

6

Club: *Liverpool*
Country: *Uruguay*

The Uruguay superstar added lethal finishing to his awesome work-rate and dribbling in 2013! He used to miss the target more often than a rubbish Call Of Duty gamer, but now he finishes off chances like an ice-cool hero!

ROBERT LEWANDOWSKI

5 BVB 09

Club: *Borussia Dortmund*
Country: *Poland*

We loved Lewandowski in 2012, but he stepped it up another level in 2013! How many strikers can say they've scored FOUR goals against Real Madrid in a Champions League semi? He's unbelievable in front of goal!

DID YOU KNOW?
LEWANDOWSKI NEARLY JOINED BLACKBURN BACK IN 2010, BUT THE MOVE DIDN'T HAPPEN AFTER HIS FLIGHT GOT CANCELLED!

DID YOU KNOW?
FALCAO BECAME THE FIRST EVER PLAYER TO SCORE A UEFA SUPER CUP HAT-TRICK AFTER BAGGING THREE GOALS AGAINST CHELSEA IN 2012!

RADAMEL FALCAO

4

Club: *Monaco*
Country: *Colombia*

Falcao has always been a quality hitman, but he's turned into a footy phenomenon over the last 18 months! He netted 28 goals in 34 La Liga starts for Atletico Madrid, then bagged a monster £51 million move to Monaco!

ROBIN VAN PERSIE

3

Club: Man. United
Country: Holland

RVP had loads of injury problems before 2011, but since then the only damage he's done is to opposition defenders! He's got one of the world's best left foots, won two Prem Golden Boots in a row and bagged his first title!

CRISTIANO RONALDO

2

Club: Real Madrid
Country: Portugal

CR7 is a footy icon! He ticks all the boxes - pace, power, long shots, free-kicks, one-on-one finishing and heading skills! He bagged the top scorer prize in the 2012-13 Champions League after smashing home 12 goals!

LIONEL MESSI

1

Club: *Barcelona*
Country: *Argentina*

Leo is the greatest footy star that's ever lived! He makes defenders cry with his dribbling and goalkeepers scream with his finishing! He netted 46 goals in 28 La Liga starts last season – we didn't think that was possible! Messi's a real-life superhero!

DID YOU KNOW?

MESSI WON THE CHAMPO LEAGUE TOP SCORER AWARD FOUR YEARS IN A ROW BETWEEN 2009 AND 2012!

HAVE YOUR SAY!

Pick your Top 10, get your dad to do one too, send them to match.magazine@ bauermedia.co.uk and we'll give a prize to the best!

Closing date: Jan. 31, 2014

MEGASTARS OF 2013

Ronaldo stopped Lionel Messi winning his fifth Champions League Top Scorer award in a row by finishing 2012-13 with 12 goals!

Portugal's legendary winger silenced his former club Man. United with two goals against The Red Devils in the Champions League!

The Real Madrid hero finished the 2012-13 season with 34 La Liga goals in just 30 starts! C-Ron had 235 shots and grabbed ten assists, too!

RONALDO

BIG MATCH! QUIZ

PREMIER LEAGUE SPECIAL

FLASHBACK!

Which Prem full-back will want to forget this dodgy old pic?

5 QUESTIONS ON...

ANDY CARROLL

WEST HAM UNITED

1 The giant West Ham striker started his career at which big north-east club – Newcastle, Sunderland or Middlesbrough?

2 True or False? The England international once had a loan spell at League 1 side Preston!

3 How much did Liverpool sign the powerful striker for back in January 2011 – £25 million, £30 million or £35 million?

4 How many Premier League goals did Andy score for The Hammers last season – five, six or seven?

5 How old is the massive England striker – 24, 25 or 26 years old?

FIFA 13 CHALLENGE!

Can you work out the names of these class Chelsea stars from FUT 13?

84 GK	
85 DIV	85 REF
81 HAN	45 SPD
75 KIC	84 POS

76 RB	
80 PAC	71 DRI
57 SHO	77 DEF
76 PAS	68 HEA

1. _____

2. _____

SOCCER SCRABBLE

Rearrange these letters to find an epic Premier League team!

C₃ P Y₄ A₁ R₁ L₁ A₁ C₃ S₁ T₁ L₁ E₁ A₁

SPOT THE BALL!

Mark where you think the ball should be in this action pic!

| | 1 | 2 | 3 | 4 | 5 | 6 | 7 | 8 | 9 | 10 | 11 | 12 | 13 | 14 | 15 | 16 | 17 | 18 | 19 |

A B C D E F G H I J K

Match these old stadiums to the clubs that played in them!

Highbury 1
Maine Road 2
The Dell 3
Roker Park 4

A Southampton
B Arsenal
C Sunderland
D Man. City

TRUE or FALSE?

Read these statements and work out if they're true or false!

1. Premier League giants Man. United are nicknamed The Black Cats!

2. Arsenal's Emirates Stadium is the second-biggest Prem stadium!

3. There are six London clubs in the 2013-14 Premier League! ✓

4. Robin van Persie was the Premier League's top scorer last season! ✓

5. Hull are the most northern Premier League team in 2013-14!

ANSWERS ON PAGE 90

THE GERRARD STORY

I'M A TOTAL FOOTY LEGEND!

MATCH LOOKS BACK AT THE LIVERPOOL STAR'S EPIC CAREER SO FAR!

STEVEN GEORGE GERRARD WAS BORN ON MAY 30, 1980! HE JOINED LIVERPOOL'S ACADEMY WHEN HE WAS NINE YEARS OLD, THEN SIGNED A PROFESSIONAL CONTRACT IN 1997 THAT WOULD CHANGE HIS LIFE FOREVER! HE MADE HIS REDS DEBUT ONE YEAR LATER, AGED 18, IN THE PREMIER LEAGUE AGAINST BLACKBURN ON NOVEMBER 29, 1998!

STEVIE G BECAME A MASSIVE STAR IN THE 2000-01 SEASON WHEN HE HELPED LIVERPOOL WIN THE FA CUP, LEAGUE CUP AND UEFA CUP TREBLE! HIS ENGLAND CAREER ALSO GOT A MAJOR BOOST IN 2001 WHEN HE NETTED A 20-YARD WONDER STRIKE TO HELP ENGLAND THRASH MEGA RIVALS GERMANY 5-1 IN MUNICH!

WHY IS RIISE WEARING MY GRANNY'S HAT?

PICK THAT ONE OUT!

GERRARD RAPIDLY BECAME LIVERPOOL'S MAIN MAN, BUT HE TURNED INTO A GLOBAL SUPERSTAR IN 2004-05! THE REDS NEEDED TO BEAT OLYMPIAKOS BY TWO GOALS TO QUALIFY FOR THE CHAMPIONS LEAGUE KNOCKOUT STAGES, AND HIS LAST-SECOND THUNDERBOLT HELPED THEM WIN 3-1!

LIVERPOOL WENT ON TO REACH THE CHAMPIONS LEAGUE FINAL THAT SEASON, BUT THEY WENT 3-0 DOWN TO ITALIAN LEGENDS AC MILAN IN ISTANBUL! GERRARD SCORED TO START THE GREATEST COMEBACK OF ALL TIME – THE REDS DREW 3-3, WON THE PENALTY SHOOT-OUT AND STEVIE LIFTED THE FAMOUS TROPHY!

"WHO'S THIS CHUMP?"

ONE YEAR AFTER THE GREATEST SEASON OF HIS LIFE CAME THE GREATEST GAME OF HIS LIFE! GERRARD BAGGED AN ASSIST AND TWO GOALS, INCLUDING A LAST-MINUTE WORLDY FROM 35 YARDS, AS THE REDS BEAT WEST HAM IN THE 2006 FA CUP FINAL!

IN 2006, GERRARD BECOME THE FIRST LIVERPOOL STAR TO WIN PFA PLAYER OF THE YEAR SINCE 1988, BUT IT ALL WENT WRONG WHEN HE MISSED A PENALTY FOR ENGLAND IN THE WORLD CUP QUARTER-FINAL AGAINST PORTUGAL!

STEVIE G BOSSED THE MIDFIELD AS LIVERPOOL BEAT BARCELONA AND CHELSEA ON THE WAY TO THE 2007 CHAMPO LEAGUE FINAL, BUT AC MILAN GOT REVENGE ON THE REDS BY BEATING THEM 2-1 IN ATHENS!

"THIS BADGE TASTES LIKE MAOAM!"

STEVIE G HAS ALWAYS LOVED PLAYING AGAINST MAN. UNITED, AND SCORED A PENALTY AS LIVERPOOL SMASHED THEIR ARCH RIVALS 4-1 AT OLD TRAFFORD IN MARCH 2009! MATCH WILL NEVER FORGET HIS CRAZY CAMERA-KISSING GOAL CELEBRATION!

THE LIVERPOOL CAPTAIN ALSO SCORED HIS FIRST PREM HAT-TRICK IN THE 5-0 WIN AGAINST ASTON VILLA IN MARCH 2009, BUT THE SEASON ENDED IN HEARTBREAK AS MAN. UNITED WON THE TITLE!

"HANDS UP IF YOU LOVE GERRARD!"

GERRARD IS STILL GOING STRONG AT 33! HE'S THE ENGLAND CAPTAIN, WON THE LEAGUE CUP IN 2012, SCORED A STUNNING HAT-TRICK AGAINST LOCAL RIVALS EVERTON ON HIS 400TH PREM APPEARANCE AND HAD HIS TESTIMONIAL BACK IN AUGUST! LEGEND!

THEO WALCOTT
ARSENAL

THEO SAYS: "I'm scared of flying! I went on a plane to Manchester, a little four-man plane, and I was absolutely terrified during that trip! We had rain, thunder, everything that day – it was so scary! The funny thing is, I deal with it by going to sleep. None of the Arsenal lads can understand how I do this, but it works! I sleep so deeply that I could probably sleep through a tornado!"

PHIL JAGIELKA
EVERTON

JAGS SAYS: "My biggest fear used to be spiders – I don't like the way they move! But now I have two kids I have to put on a brave face or I'll make them more scared than they already are! I'm the spider-catching expert in my house now – I act brave, but really I'm screaming like a little girl inside!"

FRANK LAMPARD
CHELSEA

LAMPS SAYS: "I'm a bit scared of heights! Put it this way, I don't like standing near the edge of a cliff! I sometimes get scared on aeroplanes, but it's difficult when I'm with my kids because they're excited so I have to show them I'm okay! I'll be smiling, but I'll hold onto the armrests during take-off!"

T FEAR!

KOLO TOURE
LIVERPOOL

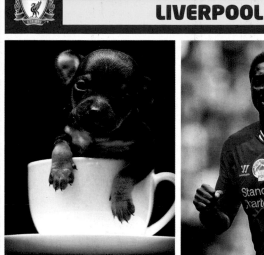

KOLO SAYS: "I'm really scared of dogs! I have a scar on my leg from when I ran away from a dog when I was a young boy and fell over. It was a really small dog and wouldn't have hurt me, but I still ran away from it! I've been scared of all dogs ever since!"

PETER CROUCH
STOKE

CROUCHY SAYS: "My biggest fear is probably claustrophobia – I hate being in tight spaces! I had a brain scan a little while ago and it was horrible – truly horrendous! You go into the scanner and it's just like being in a coffin! Getting buried alive is another of my worst fears, so I didn't like the scan!"

ROMAN PAVLYUCHENKO
LOKOMOTIV MOSCOW

PAV SAYS: "I'm absolutely terrified of flying! The biggest problem is, I have to fly a lot because of football so I try to distract myself during flights. I watch a movie or listen to some music and try not to think about it. I've also had a few team-mates in the past who've helped distract me, so I've managed to cope!"

GARY CAHILL
CHELSEA

GAZ SAYS: "I'm scared of heights! When I say heights, I mean things like standing on the edge of the Eiffel Tower with only a little railing between you and falling off! I'm not happy with stuff like that at all!"

EDIN DZEKO
MAN. CITY

EDIN SAYS: "I'm scared of God. That's definitely my main fear, and I don't like snakes either! But I don't see a lot of them in Manchester, so they're not a massive worry to me!"

LEE CATTERMOLE
SUNDERLAND

LEE SAYS: "I'm scared of really small spaces! I tried scuba diving a few years ago as I love the sea, but I didn't enjoy it because I'm a little bit claustrophobic. I'm not too keen on heights, either!"

STEVEN SAYS: "I'm scared of spiders - I developed a fear when I was growing up! If they're in the house I hate getting rid of them - sometimes my friends have to do it!"

TIM CAHILL
NEW YORK RED BULLS

TIM SAYS: "I'm not sure if I'd call it a fear, but I really hate avocados! I really don't like them! Apart from that, what you see is what you get!"

SWP SAYS: "I'm not scared of anything! I'm not really the kind of person who thinks of things in that way. I wouldn't say I'm fearless, but I'm not scared of things that can't affect me!"

World Cup BRAIN-BUSTER!

Test your knowledge on footy's big trophy!

1. Who was Holland's keeper in the 2010 World Cup Final – Maarten Stekelenburg or Edwin van der Sar?

2. Which country hosted the last World Cup in 2010 – South Africa, South Korea or Brazil?

3. Midfielder Paulinho will rock for hosts Brazil in 2014, but how much did Spurs pay for him back in July?

4. Who won the World Cup with Argentina in 1986, and managed the same country at the 2010 tournament?

5. Which Uruguay star was named Player Of The Tournament at the 2010 World Cup – Suarez or Forlan?

6. Spain, Holland, Uruguay and which other country reached the semi-finals at the 2010 World Cup?

7. True or False? Brazil have won the World Cup a record seven times!

8. Who was Spain's manager for their World Cup win in 2010?

9. Name this mystery Argentina striker who'll be one of the first names on their team sheet at World Cup 2014!

10. The 2018 World Cup will be held in which country – Russia, Qatar, Turkey or England?

1 ....
2 ....
3 ....
4 ....
5 ....
6 ....
7 ....
8 ....
9 ....
10 ....

ANSWERS ON PAGE 90

Neymar's epic goal helped Brazil hammer Spain 3-0 in the Confederations Cup final! He also scored in every group game - against Mexico, Italy and Japan!

Barcelona beat Euro rivals Real Madrid, Bayern Munich, PSG and Chelsea to sign the Samba star for a wallet-busting £48.6 million in June!

He won the Golden Ball at the Confederations Cup after being voted Player Of The Tournament. He beat Andres Iniesta and Paulinho to the award!

NEYMAR

FAMOUS FOOTY

MAN. UNITED No.7

WHO'S WORN IT?
George Best
Eric Cantona
David Beckham
Cristiano Ronaldo

United's famous No.7s are proper footy legends! Best is arguably their greatest player ever, while Cantona helped The Red Devils bag four titles in five years! Becks became the most famous footy star on the planet, and Ronaldo hit 118 goals in 292 games before being sold for a world-record transfer fee!

GEORGE BEST

ERIC CANTONA

CRISTIANO RONALDO

DAVID BECKHAM

WEST HAM No.8

SCOTT PARKER

WHO'S WORN IT?
Trevor Sinclair
Teddy Sheringham
Scott Parker

The Hammers' No.8 shirt has had some top Prem stars in it! Sinclair made goals for fun at Upton Park, and Sheringham is one of the Prem's biggest legends ever! Parker was a class act for the club and won the FWA Player Of The Year while wearing the No.8, while England striker Andy Carroll wore the number last season before switching to No.9!

TEDDY SHERINGHAM

TREVOR SINCLAIR

SHIRTS!

RONALDO 7

ARSENAL No.14

WHO'S WORN IT?
Thierry Henry

The Arsenal No.14 shirt is famous thanks to one of the greatest players ever! At his peak, Henry was the most-feared striker in the world and broke loads of records! He overtook Ian Wright's tally to become The Gunners' all-time record scorer with 228 goals, he's the third-highest scorer in Prem history and is one of only two players to win the PFA Player Of The Year two seasons in a row! Legend!

RETIRED SHIRTS!

Some clubs retire a shirt number so nobody else can wear it! Here are some of our faves!

MALAGA No.22

The Anchovies retired Isco's No.22 shirt when he left for Real Madrid because their fans loved him!

COLOGNE No.10

PODOLSKI 10

Cologne have retired the No.10 shirt while club legend Lukas Podolski is still playing!

B. MUNICH No.12

The German giants love their supporters so much, they retired the No.12 to thank the fans for being their 12th man!

SCHALKE No.7

Spain legend Raul was so good during his two-year spell at Schalke, they retired his No.7 shirt for the 2012-13 season!

CHELSEA No.25

ZOLA 25

Although it's not officially retired, nobody has worn The Blues' No.25 shirt since Gianfranco Zola left in 2003!

LES FERDINAND

NEWCASTLE No.9

WHO'S WORN IT?
Jackie Milburn
Les Ferdinand
Alan Shearer

Newcastle's No.9 is one of the most famous shirts in footy history! Milburn bagged 200 goals for The Magpies and Ferdinand hit 50, but Shearer is the club's record scorer with 206! Papiss Cisse wears it now and has netted some absolute worldies, but he's got a long way to go to match Shearer and co!

ALAN SHEARER

JACKIE MILBURN

KEVIN
KEEGAN

STEVE
McMANAMAN

LIVERPOOL No.7

WHO'S WORN IT?
Kenny Dalglish
Kevin Keegan
Steve McManaman

Legendary strikers like Rush, Fowler and Torres have worn Liverpool's No.9 shirt, but the No.7 has produced world-class stars too! Dalglish scored 172 Liverpool goals, future double Ballon d'Or winner Keegan won the FWA Player Of The Year in 1976, and McManaman destroyed defenders with his tricky dribbling skills at Anfield for nearly ten years!

KENNY
DALGLISH

DUNCAN
FERGUSON

EVERTON No.10

WHO'S WORN IT?
Andy Gray
Gary Speed
Duncan Ferguson
Mikel Arteta

Everton's No.10s rock! Gray formed a top strikeforce with lethal No.9 Graeme Sharp in the 1980s, Speed is a Prem legend and no Everton player scored more Prem goals than Ferguson! Arteta was the last star to wear it permanently, and Toffees fans will hope loan star Gerard Deulofeu can make the same impact in 2013-14!

MIKEL
ARTETA

GARY
SPEED

ANDY
GRAY

TOTTENHAM No.10

WHO'S WORN IT?
Jimmy Greaves
Glenn Hoddle
Gary Lineker
Robbie Keane

Spurs have a history of some epic No.10s! Greaves is the club's record scorer with a tally of 266 goals, Hoddle is recognised as one of the most naturally-gifted English players of all time, Lineker is one of England's most lethal striker ever, and Keane hit 122 goals in two spells at White Hart Lane!

GLENN HODDLE

ROBBIE KEANE

JIMMY GREAVES

GARY LINEKER

CHELSEA No.8

WHO'S WORN IT?
Alan Hudson
Mark Hughes
Gus Poyet
Frank Lampard

Chelsea's No.8s have always been Stamford Bridge heroes! Hudson was a Blues legend in the '60s and '70s, Hughes was a key player for Chelsea in the '90s and Poyet scored tons of goals in it! Lamps has worn the shirt since 2001, and he sealed his place in the history books after smashing Chelsea's all-time goals record!

GUS POYET

FRANK LAMPARD

MARK HUGHES

ALAN HUDSON

CRAZY NUMBERS!

Why have the stars worn these high numbers?

VICTOR WANYAMA 67

The powerful Kenya and Southampton midfielder wore the No.67 shirt when he played for Celtic to show respect for the club's famous European Cup victory of 1967!

NICOLAS ANELKA 39

Anelka wore No.39 at Man. City as No.9 was taken, and he had such a good spell that he's worn it at Fenerbahce, Bolton, Chelsea, Shanghai Shenhua, Juventus and West Brom too!

GARY HOOPER 88

Hooper is another ex-Celtic star to have worn a crazy number! MATCH heard he took the No.88 shirt because the No.10 was taken and 1988 is the year he was born!

ANTONIO CASSANO 99

Cassano's crazy shirt number is because 9+9=18 – his lucky number! He first wore it at Sampdoria because the No.18 was taken, and then took it to AC Milan, Inter and Parma!

NICKLAS BENDTNER 52

Bendtner changed his Arsenal shirt number from No.26 to No.52 in 2009, saying it was a special number to him! We've heard he wanted it because he was earning £52,000 a week at the time!

RONALDINHO 49

Ronnie wore No.49 at Atletico Mineiro as the No.10 was taken and it's the year his Mum was born! He also wore No.80 for AC Milan from 2008 to 2010 because he was born in 1980!

RU 2 BROTHERS?

Check out the best lookalikes of the year!

TROY McCLURE
THE SIMPSONS

DAVID MOYES
MAN. UNITED BOSS

FABIO COENTRAO
PORTUGAL

STACEY SOLOMON
TV HOST

LEWIS HAMILTON
F1 DRIVER

LEROY FER
NORWICH

KOBE BRYANT
NBA LEGEND

THEO WALCOTT
ARSENAL

GAIL McINTYRE
CORONATION STREET

LUKA MODRIC
REAL MADRID

RON VLAAR
ASTON VILLA

JASON STATHAM
ACTOR

Mata won Chelsea's Player Of The Year, the club's Players' Player Of The Year and was named in the PFA Team Of The Year in 2013!

The silky Spain playmaker is a creative king - he scored or assisted 49 goals in 64 games in all competitions for Chelsea in 2012-13! Legend!

Mata hit double figures for goals and assists in the Prem last season - only Wayne Rooney, Santi Cazorla and Theo Walcott did the same!

MATA

BIG MATCH! QUIZ

WORLD CUP SPECIAL

Asamoah Gyan | Wesley Sneijder | Thomas Muller | Diego Forlan

Gonzalo Higuain

David Villa

ODD ONE OUT!

Which of these stars scored less than four goals at World Cup 2010?

FLIPPED!

Which Japan superstar has had his face messed up in this weird pic?

CRAZY KIT!

Which country wore this mad strip at World Cup 94?

5 QUESTIONS ON...

DAVID LUIZ

BRASIL

1 How old is the crazy-haired Brazil defender – 23, 24, 25, 26 or 27 years old?

2 Who was his centre-back partner for Brazil in the 2013 Confederations Cup Final against Spain?

3 Chelsea bought him from which Portuguese superclub in 2011 – Benfica or Porto?

4 True or False? The classy defender started his career with La Liga giants Barcelona!

5 He scored a long-range thunderbolt against which Premier League team in April

NAME THE TEAM!

Can you remember Spain's starting XI that beat Holland in the 2010 World Cup Final?

1. Barcelona ★ Forward

2. Barcelona ★ Midfielder

3. Real Madrid ★ Right-back

Espanyol ★ Left-back
JOAN CAPDEVILA

4. Barcelona ★ Centre-back

5. Real Madrid ★ Midfielder

6. Real Madrid ★ Goalkeeper

7. Barcelona ★ Midfielder

8. Atletico Madrid ★ Striker

9. Barcelona ★ Midfielder

10. Barcelona ★ Centre-back

GUESS THE WINNERS!

Which countries won these World Cups?

1966

1998

2002

2006

World Cup Heroes!

Which countries do these stars play for?

1. Arjen Robben

2. Heung-Min Son

3. Ilkay Gundogan

4. Tim Cahill

5. Keisuke Honda

6. Luiz Gustavo

MATCH! WINNER!

Who scored Spain's winning goal in the 2010 World Cup Final against Holland?

ANSWERS ON PAGE 90

ROSS BARKLEY
EVERTON

18 78 Everton

ENGLAND

BARKLEY'S STATS!

PASSING		9
FOOTY BRAIN		8
LONG SHOTS		9
PACE		8
TACKLING		8
STRENGTH		9

BIG FACT!

Ross was a key member of the England team that beat Spain in the U17 Euro Championship Final in 2010!

EARLY YEARS!

ROSS SAYS: "I got scouted by Everton when I was 11 years old playing for my Sunday league team, Ash Celtic. I didn't feel well on the day of the trial and said maybe I should miss it, but my mum told me I'd be alright and I ended up playing well and signing!"

LOCAL SUCCESS!

ROSS SAYS: "We had some top players at my school, Broadgreen International, and we won the Liverpool Echo Cup and Merseyside Cup! We played a good school called All Saints in the final of the Echo Cup and won 3-1! I scored two, so it was a really good day."

FOOTY SKILLS!

ROSS SAYS: "If I had to describe my game, I'd say that I like playing off the striker and I'm not afraid to get the ball under pressure and drive forward. Hopefully, in a few years after gaining experience, I'll be able to play deeper and be a leader on the pitch as well!"

MEGA FACTPACK!

Full Name: Ross Barkley
Nickname: Rossi
Date Of Birth: December 5, 1993
Position: Midfielder
Club: Everton
Country: England
Top Skill: Powering past opponents!

G THING!

PERFECT POSITION!

ROSS SAYS: "The Tim Cahill No.10 position suits me, or I can play in any of the attacking midfield spots in a 4-2-3-1 formation. To play in a midfield two you need discipline, and that's something I'll learn with experience."

BIG SUPPORT!

ROSS SAYS: "Since I was young, I've always said to my mum that if I make it I'm going to be good to her. But my mum's always said, 'It's WHEN you make it, Ross, WHEN!' I obviously haven't made it yet because I need to get loads of games in the Premier League, but I'm at the start!"

BIG FACT!

Barkley started his footy life as an attack-minded centre-back!

ROLE MODELS!

ROSS SAYS: "Zinedine Zidane and Wayne Rooney are my role models! I loved Zidane's swagger and the way he made everything look easy, while Rooney came through at Everton like me, he's a Scouser and he's become one of the best players in the world!"

IN THREE YEARS...

ROSS SAYS: "I want to be playing regularly for Everton, playing good football and in the England squad! I'm very ambitious and I believe in myself, so I'd really like to have a few England caps by then!"

TURN OVER FOR MORE STARS WHO'LL ROCK 2014!

OFFICIALLY THE UK'S BEST-SELLING FOOTY ANNUAL

MATCH!

MEGA VALUE!

ANNUAL 20

NEW WORLD BEA

MARIO GOTZE
BAYERN MUNICH ★ GERMANY

Gotze left Dortmund to test himself at one of Europe's biggest clubs last summer, and that move could push him on to the next level! His footy brain, passing and one-touch play are already world class!

ISCO
REAL MADRID ★ SPAIN

Spain's latest midfield star has the talent to become Real Madrid's key player in 2014! Isco has the vision, technique and confidence to turn a match – he could become Real's answer to Andres Iniesta!

THIBAUT COURTOIS
A. MADRID ★ BELGIUM

The 21-year-old Chelsea keeper has become a star during his loan spell at Atletico Madrid! The Belgium ace won La Liga's Best Goalkeeper award last season, and could become the best shot-stopper in the world!

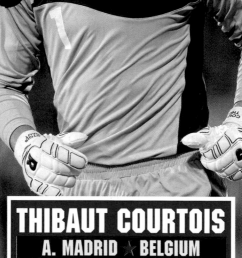

THESE KIDS AREN'T BAD EITHER!

ALEX OXLADE-CHAMBERLAIN
ARSENAL ★ ENGLAND

MARCO VERRATTI
PSG   ITALY

ALVARO MORATA
REAL MADRID ★ SPAIN

TERS...2014

MATCH reveals the wonderkids who'll rule the footy world in 2014!

WILFRIED ZAHA
MAN. UNITED ★ ENGLAND

MATCH named Zaha the Football League Player Of The Year in 2013, and we expect him to win tons more awards at United! The winger has great control, is a top dribbler and his pace gives defenders nightmares!

RAPHAEL VARANE
REAL MADRID ★ FRANCE

The France wonderkid gets better with every game! The 20-year-old centre-back pays no attention to big reputations and bosses strikers with his touch-tight marking, lightning pace and perfectly-timed tackles!

NEYMAR
BARCELONA ★ BRAZIL

European footy fans have been dreaming about seeing Neymar in Champions League action for years! The Brazil trickster's rapid pace and flash tricks mean he creates and scores goals out of nothing!

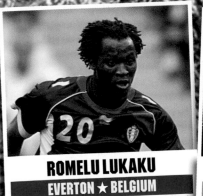

ROMELU LUKAKU
EVERTON ★ BELGIUM

BERNARD
SHAKHTAR DONETSK ★ BRAZIL

LORENZO INSIGNE
NAPOLI ITALY

JULIAN DRAXLER
SCHALKE ★ GERMANY

Championship BRAIN-BUSTER!

How much do you know about the Championship?

1. Which team finished second to Cardiff in the 2012-13 season?

2. Name the Crystal Palace striker who finished top scorer last season!

3. Which current Championship team are based the furthest north – Blackburn, Bolton or Middlesbrough?

4. Eight 2013-14 Championship team names start with the letter 'B', but only one starts with 'C' – name the club!

5. Doncaster, Bournemouth and which other team were promoted to the Championship last May?

6. Which team has the biggest stadium in the Championship – Leeds, Sheffield Wednesday or Nottingham Forest?

7. Who are this season's Championship sponsors – Sky Net, Sky Bet, Sky Set or Sky Pet?

8. Which 2013-14 Championship team play their home games at Pride Park?

9. Name the quality south-coast club who play at The AMEX and are managed by Oscar Garcia!

10. How many games does each team play in a Championship season – 38, 42 or 46?

1 ....
2 ....
3 ....
4 ....
5 ....
6 ....
7 ....
8 ....
9 ....
10 ....

ANSWERS ON PAGE 90

Suarez's tricky feet and top dribbling skills won five penalties in the Prem last season for Liverpool – that's more than any other player!

The lethal goal king became the first ever Uruguayan to be named in the Premier League Team Of The Year last season!

Luis is Uruguay's leading scorer in the 2014 World Cup qualifiers, and bagged three goals at the 2013 Confederations Cup too! He's a goal machine!

SUAREZ

BALE REVEALED!

MATCH tells you everything about the Welsh wing wizard!

BALE THROUGH THE YEARS!

SAINTS STAR!

Bale was born in Cardiff on July 16, 1989 and lived there until he was eight, before signing for Southampton's academy!

Gareth became the youngest ever Wales international when he made his debut against Trinidad & Tobago in May 2006!

FLYING DRAGON!

Gaz became Wales' youngest ever goalscorer when he whipped home a stunning free-kick against Slovakia back in October 2006! He was just 17!

2006-07

2007-08

2005-06

BABY BALE!

He went to Whitchurch High School in Cardiff with Wales and British Lions rugby captain Sam Warburton!

Gaz roomed with Arsenal's Theo Walcott when they were in The Saints' academy! Before they left the club, both stars signed the wall to make sure they weren't forgotten!

Bale made his first-team debut for Southampton against Millwall in April 2006, aged just 16 years and 275 days! He's the second-youngest ever Saints player!

BALE ON...
...getting better!

GAZ SAYS: "My right foot can improve! I scored a few goals with it last season, but they all scuttled along the floor! A lot of people show me on to my right foot now, so if I can improve I'll hopefully score more than four!"

BALE ON...
...his football hero!

GAZ SAYS: "My favourite footballer is Ryan Giggs. He was my hero when I was younger – he's Welsh, left-sided and plays a similar game to me. He's definitely my hero!"

The Wales megastar has been going out with his girlfriend Emma Rhys-Jones for years!

2008-09

Tottenham paid Southampton an initial £5 million for Bale in May 2007! They ended up paying just £7 million - is he the signing of the century?

SPURS MOVE!

2 Septiembre 2013

FACTS & STATS!

Full Name: *Gareth Frank Bale*
Age: 24 **Strongest Foot:** Left
Position: *Left wing/Forward*
Height: *6ft 1in* **Weight:** *74kg*
Club: *Real Madrid* **Country:** *Wales*
Top Skill: *Rocket long shots!*
Talent Rating: *World-class!*

WALES LEGEND!

SPEED MACHINE!

Bale wears the Adidas adizero F50 boots, and has been signed up to the massive sportswear company since 2006!

The Wales megastar has been named in the PFA Team Of The Year for the last three seasons! He won the PFA Player Of The Year award in 2011, and was named PFA Player and Young Player Of The Year in 2013!

He went on a crazy club-record run of 24 games without being on the winning side when he first joined Spurs!

The Welsh rocket has been clocked running at 22mph on the pitch, and his record time for the 100 metres is 11.5 seconds!

2011-12

2010-11

2009-10

His first child, daughter Alba Violet Bale, was born on October 21, 2012!

2012-13

HAPPY DAYS!

Gareth loves changing his shirt number! He wore No.16 in his first season at Spurs, changed to the No.3 in 2008, and switched again to No.11 at the start of last season!

Bale became a world star when he hit a Champions League hat-trick past Inter Milan in October 2010!

KING OF HEARTS!

Bale has been celebrating with a heart sign to the crowd for years, and the Wales legend has even had it trademarked!

2013-14

Gaz finally topped MATCH's Top 50 Players in the UK and Ireland in 2013 after finishing runner-up twice in 2011 and 2012!

WORLD BEATER!

Bale finally completed his dream move to Real Madrid on September 1 to become the most expensive player of all time!

If footy stars were... Pop Stars!

MATCH compares some music chart heroes to footy superstars!

I AIN'T NO PUNK, MATCH!

NO, YOU'RE JUST DAFT, HATEM!

HATEM BEN ARFA
would be...
DAFT PUNK

Ben Arfa was a star in France before bringing his quality to England - just like Daft Punk! Prem defenders need to 'Get Lucky' when they face him!

THAT HAT IS STUPID, BIEBS!

YOU'RE JUST JEALOUS, CHUMP!

NEYMAR
would be...
JUSTIN BIEBER

These are two of the most famous wonderkids on the planet! Some of their tricks annoy people and tons of critics say they're overrated, but they both sell out every arena they play in!

LAMPS IS A TOTAL STAR!

BUT JAY-Z'S LOADS RICHER!

FRANK LAMPARD
would be...
JAY-Z

These legends have been at the top for years! Younger stars try to steal their crowns, but they love silencing critics with incredible displays!

I EVEN PLAY THE GUITAR LIKE A PRO!

YOU'VE GOT NOTHING ON ME, RON!

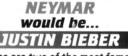

YOUR HAIR'S SHOCKING, JESS!

ERR... HELLO?

WAYNE ROONEY
would be...
JESSIE J

Wazza and JJ lost some of their star quality when they shaved their heads, but they're still top class on their day! They'll be back to their best in 2014!

CRISTIANO RONALDO
would be...
JUSTIN TIMBERLAKE

CR7 and JT both know how good they are and they don't care who knows it! Timberlake sells loads of albums and Ronaldo scores loads of goals, and they both love looking in the mirror!

Robben hit four goals in Bayern's Champions League run last season, including the winner in the final and a goal in both semis against Barcelona!

The tricky Bayern Munich and Holland winger scored 13 goals and grabbed 10 assists in just 23 starts in all comps in 2012-13!

Robben averaged four shots per game in last season's Champions League - that was more than Lionel Messi and Robert Lewandowski!

ROBBEN

BIG MATCH! QUIZ

CHAMPIONSHIP SPECIAL

crazy names!

Which Championship teams have these nicknames?

1. Glovers

2. Owls

3. Terriers

4. Blues

5. Tykes

6. Cherries

TRUE or FALSE?

Read these statements and work out if they're true or false!

1. Three Championship teams get automatic promotion to the Prem!

2. Middlesbrough, Barnsley, Charlton and Nottingham Forest's home shirts are red!

3. Championship giants Blackburn play their home games at Ewood Road!

4. Watford lost in last season's Championship play-off final!

5. Millwall are the only London club playing in the Championship in 2013-14!

CAMERA SHY!

Can you name the Championship bosses hiding in these pics?

CHAMPIONSHIP HEROES!

A — Leicester — LEICESTER CITY FOOTBALL CLUB

B — Bolton

C — Blackburn — BLACKBURN ROVERS F.C. 18 75 ARTE ET LABORE

Jermaine Beckford
1

David Dunn
2

Anthony Knockaert
3

Match these Championship stars to the clubs they play for!

MYSTERY MASCOT!

Use the clues below to work out which club this mascot comes from!

↘ I appear with my cool mascot mate Belle on matchdays at St. Andrew's!

↘ My team, Blues, beat Prem giants Arsenal to win the League Cup back in 2011!

↘ I'm big pals with Wade Elliott and Paul Robinson!

5 QUESTIONS ON...
LEEDS

1 Where do the massive Yorkshire club play their home games – Elland Road, Riverside Stadium, Oakwell, Turf Moor or The Den?

2 Who is the current United manager – Bob McTavish, Brian McDermott or Barry McIntosh?

3 True or False? They last won the top-flight league title in 1992!

4 Which current Man. United star joined The Red Devils from The Whites for £30 million in 2002 – Rio Ferdinand or Wayne Rooney?

5 Who was Leeds' top scorer in 2012 13 Luciano Becchio, Ross McCormack or El Hadji Diouf?

2013

2012

GUESS THE WINNERS!
Who won the Championship title in these seasons?

2011

2010

ANDREWS HEAT FOR HIRE

1.

buy mobiles .net

2.

wonga.com

3.

🔍 SPOT THE SPONSOR!
Which Championship teams have these sponsors on their shirts?

KING POWER

4.

AirAsia

5.

壹贰博 12BET

6.

BACK TO THE FUTURE

Which Championship boss is pictured here with music legend Elvis Presley?

ANSWERS ON PAGE 90

TOP 10

BEST-PAID PLAYERS!

10

MESSI
£170,000 PER WEEK
Leo's one of the best players of all time, but he's only tenth in the pay league! We've heard mega-rich PSG would love to make him the world's best-paid player, but there's no sign of him leaving Barcelona just yet!

9

CONCA
£175,000 PER WEEK
Hands up who's heard of this guy? We thought so! The tiny attacking midfielder was one of the best players in the Brazilian league in 2011 before Chinese super club Guangzhou swooped to sign him! He pockets bundles of cash!

7=

TORRES
£180,000 PER WEEK
Chelsea paid a British record £50 million to sign Torres in 2011 and made him their best-paid star! The Spain striker has struggled to live up to his huge price tag, but there are signs El Nino's starting to rediscover his old form again!

7=

VAN PERSIE
£180,000 PER WEEK
RVP's £24 million move to United lifted him into the top division of footy star earners! Man. City are rumoured to have offered him £230,000 a week, but his Prem winner's medal will make up for the £50k-a-week loss!

6

AGUERO
£205,000 PER WEEK
Man. City rolled out the big bucks for Sergio Aguero in 2011 and he's been worth every penny! Kun's one of the most-feared strikers in the Prem, and no-one will ever forget his last-gasp title winning strike against QPR!

5

YAYA TOURE
£215,000 PER WEEK

Toure is a tank of a player, and getting that powerful costs a lot of money! We've heard the City hero spends chunks of his mega wages on fish, chicken and pasta to stay in top condition for bossing midfield opponents!

4

ROONEY
£230,000 PER WEEK

Wazza was involved in one of the biggest transfer stories of last summer, but rumours about him leaving Old Trafford were nothing to do with his wages! The England ace earns so much money he could buy a new Ferrari every week!

3

IBRAHIMOVIC
£240,000 PER WEEK

Ligue 1 was famous for paying tiny wages for years, but that all changed when Qatari billionaires QIA bought PSG! They made Sweden hero Zlatan Ibrahimovic their star player and the third best-paid footballer in the world!

1

FALCAO
£300,000 PER WEEK

The Colombia striker made his mega-bucks move to Monaco back in May and signed an epic five-year, £78.5 million contract! El Tigre just edges out Bale as the best-paid player in the world, because he pays next to nothing in tax and pockets nearly all his wages!

2

BALE
£300,000 PER WEEK

Everyone knew Bale was on his way to Madrid months before the deal was finally completed, but even MATCH is surprised at the money he's now getting! He's earning more than three times the amount he was at Spurs!

THE LAMPARD STORY

MATCH LOOKS BACK AT THE CHELSEA LEGEND'S INCREDIBLE CAREER!

YOU'D BETTER BE AS GOOD AS ME, SON!

FRANK JAMES LAMPARD WAS BORN ON JUNE 20, 1978! THE SON OF FRANK LAMPARD SNR, A WEST HAM LEGEND, THE YOUNGER LAMPARD ROCKED AT SCHOOL BEFORE DECIDING TO PLAY PROFESSIONAL FOOTBALL! HE JOINED THE HAMMERS' YOUTH TEAM IN 1994 AND MADE HIS FIRST-TEAM DEBUT IN JANUARY 1996!

LAMPARD HIT THE BIG TIME IN THE 1998-99 SEASON, WHEN HIS TOP FORM HELPED WEST HAM FINISH FIFTH IN THE PREM AND SEAL A EUROPEAN SPOT! HE ALSO WON HIS FIRST ENGLAND CALL-UP, AND MADE HIS DEBUT AGAINST BELGIUM. THE NEXT SEASON FRANK STEPPED IT UP A GEAR, SMASHING HOME 14 GOALS FROM MIDFIELD!

IT'S PARTY TIME, WAZZA!

I CAN'T HOLD THIS POSE FOREVER!

NOW A PREM STAR, FRANK BAGGED AN £11 MILLION MOVE TO CHELSEA IN 2001! THE MOVE WASN'T AN IMMEDIATE SUCCESS, BUT HE WORKED HARD TO PROVE HIMSELF TO THE BLUES' FANS. HE ALSO CONTINUED TO MAKE WAVES AT INTERNATIONAL LEVEL, AND BAGGED HIS FIRST GOAL FOR THE THREE LIONS AGAINST CROATIA IN 2003!

LAMPS HELPED CHELSEA FINISH SECOND IN THE PREMIER LEAGUE AND REACH THE CHAMPIONS LEAGUE SEMI-FINALS IN 2003-04! HE BAGGED DOUBLE FIGURES FOR LEAGUE GOALS FOR THE FIRST TIME AND MADE THE PFA TEAM OF THE YEAR! THAT SUMMER, HE HIT THREE GOALS FOR ENGLAND AT EURO 2004 BEFORE THEY WERE KNOCKED OUT IN THE QUARTER-FINALS BY PORTUGAL!

NOW I'M A PROPER LEDGE!

THE AWESOME CHELSEA MIDFIELDER HAD AN EPIC 2005! HE HELPED THE BLUES WIN THEIR FIRST TOP-FLIGHT ENGLISH TITLE FOR 50 YEARS, WAS NAMED THE PREM PLAYER OF THE YEAR AND FINISHED RUNNER-UP IN THE FIFA WORLD PLAYER OF THE YEAR AND BALLON D'OR AWARDS! LIFE COULDN'T GET MUCH BETTER FOR LAMPS!

LAMPS WENT GOAL CRAZY IN 2005-06! HIS RED-HOT FORM HELPED CHELSEA TO THEIR SECOND PREMIER LEAGUE TITLE, AND BOSS JOSE MOURINHO CALLED HIM 'THE BEST PLAYER IN THE WORLD'. IN 2007, LAMPARD SCORED SIX GOALS IN CHELSEA'S RUN TO THE FA CUP FINAL, THEN WON MAN OF THE MATCH IN THE 1-0 WIN OVER MAN. UNITED!

IN 2008, SUPER FRANK SIGNED A £40 MILLION FIVE-YEAR DEAL AT STAMFORD BRIDGE, AND CELEBRATED BY BAGGING HIS 100TH PREM GOAL JUST WEEKS LATER! HE CONTINUED TO RIP UP THE PREM AND CHAMPIONS LEAGUE, AND MADE HIS MARK ON THE FA CUP AGAIN BY HITTING THE WINNER IN THE 2009 FINAL AGAINST EVERTON AT WEMBLEY!

I HOPE NO-ONE SPOTTED IT...

LAMPARD STARTED 2009-10 BY BAGGING IN THE COMMUNITY SHIELD AGAINST MAN. UNITED, AND ENDED IT BY WINNING HIS THIRD PREM TITLE! HE ADDED AN FA CUP WINNERS' MEDAL AS THE BLUES WON THE DOUBLE, AND FINISHED THE SEASON WITH 27 GOALS IN ALL COMPS! BUT THERE WAS DISAPPOINTMENT AS HE SAW A GOAL DISALLOWED AGAINST GERMANY AT THE 2010 WORLD CUP, AND ENGLAND CRASHED OUT!

I'LL BE SLEEPING WITH THIS TONIGHT!

BY 2012, LAMPS WAS A CHELSEA HERO AND A FOOTBALL LEGEND! HE DROVE THE BLUES PAST BARCELONA IN THE CHAMPIONS LEAGUE SEMIS, BEFORE FIRING HOME A PENALTY IN THE SHOOT-OUT WIN AGAINST BAYERN MUNICH IN THE FINAL!

FRANK STARTED 2012-13 STRUGGLING WITH INJURY, BUT GOT BACK FIT AND WENT ON AN EPIC GOALSCORING RUN AFTER CHRISTMAS, BREAKING THE BLUES' ALL-TIME SCORING RECORD AND HELPING THEM WIN THE EUROPA LEAGUE! HE BAGGED A NEW ONE-YEAR DEAL AND CLOSED IN ON HIS 100TH ENGLAND CAP!

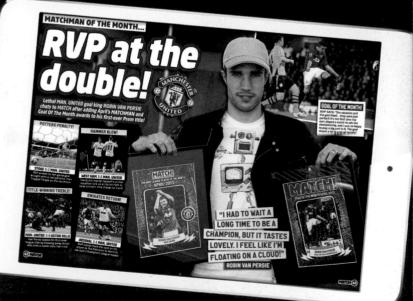

BRAZIL 2014
THE BIGGEST WORLD CUP EVER!

MATCH checks out why this summer's World Cup in Brazil could be the biggest football party of all time!

BRAZIL LOVES FOOTY!

WORK'S OUT!

The national team is such a big deal in Brazil, work places and banks shut three hours before international matches to let fans go home and get ready for the footy!

THE BIRTH OF FOOTBALL!

Football was introduced to Brazil by Scottish footy fan Thomas Donohue. The first match was played in Bangu in Brazil in April 1894, and the Brazilian Football Federation was founded 20 years later in 1914!

FAMOUS KIT!

Brazil's yellow, blue, white and green colours make up the most famous kit in footy! Brazil's shirts used to be white, but after defeat to Uruguay in the 1950 World Cup Final they were changed and the strip called 'The Little Canary' was born!

WORLD TRAVELLERS!

Brazil are the only team to have won the World Cup on four different continents! They've lifted the famous trophy in Europe at Sweden 1958, South America at Chile 1962, North America at Mexico 1970 and USA 1994, and Asia at South Korea & Japan 2002! They've never won the tournament on home soil, though – they lost the 1950 final to Uruguay!

THE GREATEST TEAM!

Brazil's 1970 World Cup-winning team is often called the greatest footballing side ever! Legendary Brazilians Jairzinho, Tostao, Carlos Alberto and Pele ripped teams to pieces before hammering Italy 4-1 in the final!

FOOTBALL SUPERPOWER!

SUPER CLUBS!

A recent survey revealed that over 33 million Brazilians support Rio de Janeiro giants Flamengo, putting them just ahead of Sao Paulo's Corinthians as the best-supported club in Brazil! Santos are the most successful club, with eight Brazilian championships!

Brazil are the most successful team in World Cup history with five wins! They're also the only country to have qualified for all 20 World Cups!

PELE!

Brazil has produced some of the best footballers of all time – none more so than Pele! The legendary striker is a footy icon, inspires youngsters and is one of the biggest reasons why Brazilians love footy so much!

THE NATIONAL GAME!

Brazilians are so footy-crazy, they'll play anywhere - on indoor five-a-side pitches, beaches or even the streets! Brazil currently has over 10,000 professional footballers all over the world!

BRAZIL-IANT FACTS!

DEADLY CREATURES!

The world's best footballers will need to watch out for some of the scariest creatures on earth! Brazil is home to the Goliath bird-eating tarantula, the second largest spider in the world! There are also tons of deadly snakes like the massive Anaconda, which can grow up to 11 metres long, plus Boa constrictors, Pit Vipers and more!

POP STARS!

Brazilians love all kinds of music, from heavy metal to reggaeton and hip hop! Daft Punk and Bruno Mars have had big hits in Brazil recently, as well as Brazilian guitarist Luan Santana and Gusttavo Lima, whose most famous video featured Neymar!

CRAZY FOOD!

Feijoada is the national dish of Brazil! It's a stew of beans, salted pig's ears, tail and feet, bacon, pork ribs, beef and cow's tongue mixed with cabbage, potatoes, carrots, pumpkin and sometimes even banana!

Brazil is famous for its footy, but there are loads of other crazy things it's known for! Check out these bonkers facts!

THE JUNGLE!

Almost half of Brazil is covered by rainforest, and there are areas the size of the UK that haven't been explored yet! The Amazon is the second largest river in the world, flowing through thousands of miles of jungle, and experts reckon there are at least 60 tribes there who've not made contact with the outside world!

SAMBA MOVES!

The word you'll hear more than any other at Brazil 2014 is 'Samba'! The whole of Brazil is obsessed with its catchy tunes and butt-shaking dance moves! It's so big, thousands of people even go to samba schools full-time to improve their dancing skills!

RIO CARNIVAL!

Brazilians love dancing and dressing up in crazy costumes, which is why the Rio Carnival has become the biggest street party in the world! The festival takes place before Lent every year, and a mind-blowing two million people fill the streets every day!

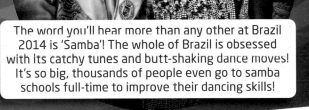

NEW SPORTS!

Football is easily the most popular sport in Brazil, but others are starting to learn a few lessons from the world's best game! Volleyball has become really popular with teenagers who like to play 'Footvolley', where players use their feet and head to get the ball over the net!

BRAZIL SUPERSTARS!

THIAGO SILVA

CENTRE-BACK
PSG

The solid star is probably the best centre-back in the world right now! His huge £35 million move to PSG in 2012 made him the most expensive defender ever!

GARRINCHA

WINGER
1955-66

Garrincha's nickname was the 'Angel With Bent Legs', but that didn't stop him sprinting with the ball like a total legend! The pocket rocket is famous for being one of the best dribblers of all time – his tricks made defenders look silly!

OSCAR

ATTACKING MIDFIELDER
CHELSEA

Chelsea's little magician pops up where defenders least expect him to and he's always causing trouble! His long shots, movement and rapid one-twos are lethal weapons!

ROMARIO

STRIKER
1987-2005

Romario hit 55 goals in just 70 games and is one of the most lethal strikers of all time! His movement, first touch and shooting were all off the charts – he loved turning on the afterburners to skin defenders, before ripping the net with his ice-cool finishing!

HULK

FORWARD
ZENIT

The awesome goal machine isn't named after The Incredible Hulk for nothing! He bosses defenders with his monster strength, and his left foot is like a sledgehammer!

DAVID LUIZ

CENTRE-BACK
CHELSEA

Luiz's best position is at centre-back, but his ability on the ball, passing, free-kicks and shooting mean he can slot into midfield too! His all-round game rocks!

NEYMAR

STRIKER
BARCELONA

Expect the unexpected when Neymar gets on the ball! The tricky Brazil goal machine has tons of natural ability and even more imagination, so anything is possible!

RONALDO

STRIKER
1994-2011

Ron's finishing and pace destroyed teams! He scored 62 goals for Brazil between 1994 and 2006, won two World Cups, is the record World Cup finals goalscorer and bagged his 98th cap in a farewell match in 2011!

PELE

STRIKER
1957-71

Pele became the youngest ever World Cup player when he starred for Brazil at the 1958 finals, aged just 17 years old! He went on to score a hat-trick in the semi-final and a double in the final, which saw him bag his first of three World Cup winners' medals! His footy brain, heading and goalscoring were out of this world, which is why he's one of the best players of all time!

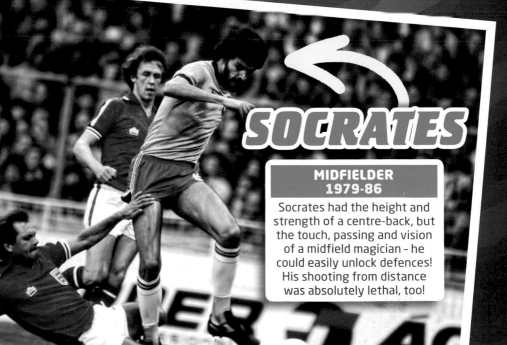

SOCRATES

MIDFIELDER
1979-86

Socrates had the height and strength of a centre-back, but the touch, passing and vision of a midfield magician – he could easily unlock defences! His shooting from distance was absolutely lethal, too!

WORLD CUP 2014!

THE COUNTRY!

Brazil is the fifth most populated country in the world with over 190 million people! Most of the country is four hours behind British Summer Time, so games will kick off at lunchtime or in the afternoon. It'll be winter when the World Cup's on, but it only gets really cold south of Rio de Janeiro so it'll still be pretty hot!

OFFICIAL POSTER!

Check out the official Brazil 2014 poster! The colours and patterns represent the nation's culture, and the players' legs challenging for the ball reveal the map of Brazil!

2014
FIFA World Cup
Brazil™

12 June – 13 July

FIFA WORLD CUP
Brazil

GREAT GAMES!

A total of 64 kick-ass games will be played during Brazil 2014! The first game of the tournament kicks off with the hosts in Sao Paulo on June 12 at 9pm BST, while the final will take place on July 13 at The Maracana at 8pm BST!

BRILLIANT BALL!

Adidas have already designed the amazing Brazuca ball that'll be used at the World Cup! Keep checking out MATCH's Hot Stuff section for a massive review of the lightning-quick ball and loads more cool World Cup gear!

brazuca

FIFA WORLD CUP
Brazil
adidas

OFFICIAL PARTNER

I NEED TICKETS FOR THE FINAL!

GOAL-LINE TECHNOLOGY!

Brazil 2014 will be the first time ever that goal-line technology will be used at a World Cup! FIFA decided to introduce it after Frank Lampard 'scored' a ghost goal for England in the 4-1 battering by Germany at World Cup 2010 – hopefully it'll cut out all the dodgy refereeing decisions!

ARMOURED MASCOT!

You'll be able to see Fuleco, Brazil 2014's official mascot, messing about at every World Cup stadium next summer! A total of 1.7 million fans voted for the rock-hard armadillo to be the mascot, and decided his name would be a cross between football and ecologyl

SICK STADIUMS!

There are 12 stadiums in cities all over Brazil that will host World Cup games. The world-famous Maracana, which has been updated for Brazil 2014, is the biggest and holds 76,935! There are four other venues being updated, six slick, brand-new stadiums, and Brasilia's Estadio Nacional Mane Garrincha has been knocked down and rebuilt!

JUST THE TICKET!

Want to watch a live World Cup game in Brazil? Well, if you can afford the air fare, there are 3.3 million tickets available for games, ranging from around £58 for group games to a massive £635 for the final!

Champions League BRAIN-BUSTER!

Test yourself on footy's biggest club competition!

1. Real Madrid have won more CL titles than anyone else, but which club is the second-most successful?

2. Which mega-talented striker finished last season as PSG's top CL goalscorer?

3. True or False? Aston Villa and Nottingham Forest have both been crowned European Champions!

4. Which La Liga club did Man. City gaffer Manuel Pellegrini manage in the Champions League last season?

5. Which CL club won the Belgian league last season - Anderlecht, Bruges or Standard Liege?

6. Scottish champions Celtic played Elfsborg in this season's CL qualifiers, but what country are they from?

7. In which position did Champions League legends Marseille finish in Ligue 1 in 2012-13?

8. Which Real Madrid star was the only player to be sent off twice in last season's Champions League?

9. How old was PSG wonderkid Lucas Moura when the Champions League group stages kicked off this season?

10. Name the Ukraine giants who reached last season's Champions League knockout stages!

1 ....
2 ....
3 ....
4 ....
5 ....
6 ....
7 ....
8 ....
9 ....
10 ....

ANSWERS ON PAGE 90

Falcao's massive £51 million move from Atletico Madrid to French giants Monaco back in May set a new Ligue 1 transfer record!

The Colombia superhero hit 28 goals in just 34 La Liga games for Atletico last season – only Lionel Messi and Cristiano Ronaldo bagged more!

Falcao hit two hat-tricks in 2012-13 – one each against Athletic Bilbao and Chelsea – and also smashed five goals in one game past Deportivo!

FALCAO

MEGASTARS' SUPER C

Jack Wilshere
ARSENAL
Ferrari 458 Italia

ENGINE: 4.5 litre
TOP SPEED: 202mph
0-60MPH: 3.4 seconds
VALUE: £178,526
HOT or NOT ★★★★★

Fernando Torres
CHELSEA
Aston Martin DB9

ENGINE: 5.9 litre
TOP SPEED: 183mph
0-60MPH: 4.6 seconds
VALUE: £143,080
HOT or NOT ★★★★★

Wayne Rooney
MAN. UNITED
Range Rover Sport Overfinch

ENGINE: 5 litre
TOP SPEED: 140mph
0-60MPH: 5.1 seconds
VALUE: £106,390
HOT or NOT ★★☆☆☆

...ARS!

Cesc Fabregas
BARCELONA
Audi R8

ENGINE: 5.2 litre
TOP SPEED: 193mph
0-60MPH: 3.8 seconds
VALUE: £158,145
HOT or NOT ★★★★☆

ASHLEY COLE
CHELSEA
Mercedes SL63 AMG

ENGINE: 5.4 litre
TOP SPEED: 165mph
0-60MPH: 4.3 seconds
VALUE: £110,785
HOT or NOT ★★★★☆

Nemanja Vidic
MAN. UNITED
Mercedes M Class

ENGINE: 5.4 litre
TOP SPEED: 155mph
0-60MPH: 4.8 seconds
VALUE: £83,655
HOT or NOT ★★★☆☆

Lionel Messi
BARCELONA
Maserati GranTurismo

ENGINE: 4.7 litre
TOP SPEED: 188mph
0-60MPH: 4.5 seconds
VALUE: £110,110
HOT or NOT ★★★★☆

Shinji Kagawa
MAN. UNITED
Chevrolet Camaro

ENGINE: 6.2 litre
TOP SPEED: 155mph
0-60MPH: 5.6 seconds
VALUE: £41,820
HOT or NOT ★★★★★

Steven Gerrard
LIVERPOOL
Jaguar XKR

ENGINE: 5 litre
TOP SPEED: 155mph
0-60MPH: 4.6 seconds
VALUE: £84,965
HOT or NOT ★★★★

Cristiano Ronaldo
REAL MADRID
Lamborghini Aventador

12.45

ENGINE: 6.4 litre
TOP SPEED: 217mph
0-60MPH: 2.9 seconds
VALUE: £288,840
HOT or NOT ★★★★★

Emmanuel Adebayor
TOTTENHAM
Fisker Karma

ENGINE: 2 litre
TOP SPEED: 125mph
0-60MPH: 5.9 seconds
VALUE: £80,000
HOT or NOT ★★★★★

Didier Drogba
GALATASARAY
Mercedes SLR McLaren Roadster

ENGINE: 6.2 litre
TOP SPEED: 197mph
0-60MPH: 3.8 seconds
VALUE: £176,985
HOT or NOT ★★★★★

Gareth Bale
REAL MADRID
Mercedes SLS AMG

ENGINE: 6.2 litre
TOP SPEED: 197mph
0-60MPH: 3.8 seconds
VALUE: £168,485
HOT or NOT ★★★★☆

Mario Balotelli
AC MILAN
Ferrari F12 Berlinetta

ENGINE: 5.9 litre
TOP SPEED: 191mph
0-60MPH: 4.3 seconds
VALUE: £150,000
HOT or NOT ★★★★☆

Stephen Ireland
STOKE
Audi R8

ENGINE: 5.2 litre
TOP SPEED: 198mph
0-60MPH: 3.8 seconds
VALUE: £125,810
HOT or NOT ★★★★☆

Diego Lugano
WEST BROM
Aston Martin DBS

ENGINE: 5.9 litre
TOP SPEED: 191mph
0-60MPH: 4.3 seconds
VALUE: £150,000
HOT or NOT ★★★★☆

Nathan Dyer
SWANSEA
Mercedes C63 AMG Coupe

Tel: 0845 688 7288
Yiannimize
REFINED
www.yiannimize-refined.com

ENGINE: 6.2 litre
TOP SPEED: 174mph
0-60MPH: 4.2 seconds
VALUE: £58,165
HOT or NOT ★★★☆☆

Jose Enrique
LIVERPOOL
Porsche Cayenne

ENGINE: 4.8 litre
TOP SPEED: 162mph
0-60MPH: 5.7 seconds
VALUE: £68,117
HOT or NOT ★★★☆☆

All of the car stats are for the top specification of the models featured

WIN THE WORLD CUP!

Can you go all the way from the playground to the World Cup final? Use some coins as counters, grab a dice and battle your mates in this epic football board game!

37 LEGEND! You hit a hat-trick in the World Cup semi-final! Move forward three spaces!

38

39 FAIL! You pick up an ankle injury in the World Cup semi-final! Move back five spaces!

40

41 FAIL! You miss a penalty in the World Cup final! Move back nine spaces!

WINNER! YOU'RE A FOOTY LEGEND! YOU'VE WON THE WORLD CUP!

36

35 LEGEND! You're named in your country's squad for the World Cup! Move forward one space!

34

33 FAIL! You pick up a calf injury just before the World Cup! Move back five spaces!

32

31

25 FAIL! You're sent off against your team's local rivals! Move back six spaces!

26

27 LEGEND! You help your team win the Premier League title! Move forward four spaces!

28

29

30 LEGEND! You score the winning goal in the Champions League final! Move forward four spaces!

24 LEGEND! A top-four Premier League team spends £5 million on you! Move forward two spaces!

23

22

21 LEGEND! MATCH puts a big poster of you in the mag! Move forward two spaces!

20 FAIL! You hand in a transfer request after getting too big for your boots! Move back one space!

19

13

14 LEGEND! A big Championship team signs you up! Move forward two spaces!

15 FAIL! The fans are annoyed after you say you want a move to the Prem! Move back two spaces!

16

17 FAIL! You miss a penalty in the play-off semi-final! Move back four spaces!

18 LEGEND! You score a last-minute winner in the play-off final! Move forward four spaces!

12 FAIL! Your manager fines you a week's wages for missing training! Move back four spaces!

11 FAIL! You miss a last-minute penalty in the League Cup! Move back one space!

10

9 LEGEND! A League 1 team signs you up after a great run of form! Move forward one space!

8

7

START KICK-OFF! The player who rolls the highest number goes first!

2

3

4 FAIL! A scout comes to watch you play, but you have a total shocker! Move back two spaces!

5

6 LEGEND! A League 2 team offers you a contract after a great trial! Move forward one space!

Bale was voted PFA Player and Young Player Of The Year in 2012-13! He's only the third player ever to win both awards in the same season!

Bale's tally of 21 Prem goals in 2012-13 is a joint-record for Spurs in a season! It equalled Teddy Sheringham's total from 1992-93!

The Wales ace was linked with Real Madrid for ages, and finally sealed a world record £85.3 million move to The Bernabeu on September 1!

BALE

SNAPPED!

BEST OF 2013 SPECIAL! PART TWO!

Torres has to be the worst hide-and-seek player of all time!

Sporting Lisbon's Zezinho only washes his socks once a season!

Aguero prays every time he feels the need to guff!

BIG MATCH! QUIZ

CHAMPIONS LEAGUE SPECIAL

FOOTY AT THE FILMS!

Which Champo League legend has quit footy to play Kick-Ass?

MATCH! WINNER!

Who scored all four goals when Dortmund smashed Real Madrid 4-1 in the first leg of last season's Champo League semi-final?

switch!

Which Champions League superstar has taken up wrestling?

TRUE or FALSE?

Read these statements and work out if they're true or false!

1. No English clubs qualified for the quarter-finals in the 2012-13 season!

2. Ajax gaffer Frank de Boer won the Champo League as a player in 1995!

3. German clubs finished top in all of their Champions League groups in 2012-13!

4. Rafa Benitez has won the Champions League as gaffer of three different clubs!

5. Barcelona legend Lionel Messi was last season's Champions League top scorer!

SPOT THE SPONSOR!

Which Champo League teams have these names on their shirts?

Jeep **1.**	QATAR AIRWAYS **2.**	Fly Emirates **3.**
TÜRK TELEKOM **4.**	AZERBAIJAN LAND OF FIRE **5.**	AON **6.**

NAME THE TEAM!

Name Bayern Munich's starting XI that smashed Barcelona 3-0 at the Nou Camp last season!

1. Germany ★ Goalkeeper

2. Croatia ★ Striker

3. Spain ★ Midfielder

4. Belgium ★ Centre-back

5. Germany ★ Centre-back

6. Austria ★ Left-back

France ★ Winger
FRANCK RIBERY

7. Germany ★ Right-back

8. Germany ★ Midfielder

9. Holland ★ Winger

10. Germany ★ Midfielder

Match these cool stadiums to the clubs who play there!

Estadio Dragao	Estadio da Luz	The Bernabeu	Stamford Bridge
1	2	3	4

A	B	C	D
Benfica	Chelsea	Real Madrid	Porto

FREAKY FACES!

Which Prem midfielder has had his face messed up in this weird pic?

MANCHESTER UNITED   MANCHESTER UNITED

ANSWERS ON PAGE 90

QUIZ ANSWERS!

Premier League Brain-Buster Page 16

1. Reading; 2. Three - Robin van Persie, Luis Suarez & Gareth Bale; 3. Blackburn; 4. Alan Shearer; 5. 46; 6. Teddy Sheringham; 7. Barclays; 8. 38; 9. Juan Mata; 10. Cardiff.

Premier League Special Page 32-33

Flashback: Pablo Zabaleta.

Andy Carroll Quiz: 1. Newcastle; 2. True; 3. £35 million; 4. Seven; 5. 24 years old.

FIFA 13 Challenge:
1. Petr Cech; 2. Cesar Azpilicueta.

Soccer Scrabble: Crystal Palace.

Spot The Ball: G2.

Stadium Game: Highbury - Arsenal; Maine Road - Man. City; The Dell - Southampton; Roker Park - Sunderland.

True or False?:
1. False - they're The Red Devils; 2. True; 3. True; 4. True; 5. False - it's Newcastle.

World Cup Brain-Buster Page 40

1. Maarten Stekelenburg; 2. South Africa; 3. £17 million; 4. Diego Maradona; 5. Diego Forlan; 6. Germany; 7. False; 8. Vicente del Bosque; 9. Gonzalo Higuain; 10. Russia.

World Cup Special Page 48-49

Odd One Out: Asamoah Gyan.

Flipped: Shinji Kagawa.

Crazy Kit: USA.

David Luiz Quiz: 1. 26 years old; 2. Thiago Silva; 3. Benfica; 4. False; 5. Fulham.

Name The Team:
1. Pedro; 2. Sergio Busquets; 3. Sergio Ramos; 4. Gerard Pique; 5. Xabi Alonso; 6. Iker Casillas; 7. Andres Iniesta; 8. David Villa; 9. Xavi; 10. Carles Puyol.

Guess The Winners: 1966 - England; 1998 - France; 2002 - Brazil; 2006 - Italy.

World Cup Heroes:
1. Holland; 2. South Korea; 3. Germany; 4. Australia; 5. Japan; 6. Brazil.

Match Winner: Andres Iniesta.

Championship Brain-Buster Page 54

1. Hull; 2. Glenn Murray; 3. Middlesbrough; 4. Charlton; 5. Yeovil; 6. Sheff. Wednesday; 7. Sky Bet; 8. Derby; 9. Brighton; 10. 46.

Championship Special Page 62-63

Camera Shy: Gianfranco Zola, Mick McCarthy & Owen Coyle.

Crazy Names:
1. Yeovil; 2. Sheff. Wed.; 3. Huddersfield; 4. Birmingham; 5. Barnsley; 6. Bournemouth.

Championship Heroes:
Leicester - Anthony Knockaert; Bolton - Jermaine Beckford; Blackburn - David Dunn.

True or False?: 1. False - it's two; 2. True; 3. False - it's Ewood Park; 4. True; 5. False - Charlton and QPR are also London clubs.

Mystery Mascot:
Birmingham's Beau Brummie.

Leeds Quiz:
1. Elland Road; 2. Brian McDermott; 3. True; 4. Rio Ferdinand; 5. Luciano Becchio.

Guess The Winners: 2013 - Cardiff; 2012 - Reading; 2011 - QPR; 2010 - Newcastle.

Spot The Sponsor: 1. Charlton; 2. Derby; 3. Blackpool; 4. Leicester; 5. QPR; 6. Wigan.

Back To The Future: Harry Redknapp.

Champions League Brain-Buster Page 78

1. AC Milan; 2. Zlatan Ibrahimovic; 3. True; 4. Malaga; 5. Anderlecht; 6. Sweden; 7. 2nd; 8. Arbeloa 9. 21; 10. Shakhtar Donetsk.

Champions League Special Page 88-89

Footy At The Films: Andrea Pirlo.

Match Winner: Robert Lewandowski.

Sport Switch: Edinson Cavani.

True or False?: 1. True; 2. True; 3. True; 4. False - he's won it once with Liverpool; 5. False - it was Cristiano Ronaldo.

Spot The Sponsor: 1. Juventus; 2. Barcelona; 3. Arsenal; 4. Galatasaray; 5. Atletico Madrid; 6. Man. United.

Name The Team: 1. Manuel Neuer; 2. Mario Mandzukic; 3. Javi Martinez; 4. Daniel van Buyten; 5. Jerome Boateng; 6. David Alaba; 7. Philipp Lahm; 8. Thomas Muller; 9. Arjen Robben; 10. Bastian Schweinsteiger.

Stadium Game: Estadio Dragao - Porto; Estadio da Luz - Benfica; The Bernabeu - Real Madrid; Stamford Bridge - Chelsea.

Freaky Faces: Shinji Kagawa.

One point per correct answer!
MY SCORE /151

Lionel Messi won his sixth La Liga title back in May! His goals and assists helped Barça finish 15 points clear of arch rivals Real Madrid!

The Barcelona star netted 46 La Liga goals in just 28 starts in the 2012-13 season - that's nearly two goals a game! He's a total freak!

Argentina's legendary goal machine won the Ballon d'Or award for the fourth year in a row back in January! He's the world's greatest!

MESSI

FOR £1

WIN!

SUBSCRIBE TO MATCH USING THE CODE AN14 AND BE IN WITH A CHANCE OF WINNING...

PLAYSTATION 4

OR

XBOX ONE

3 GREAT REASONS TO SUBSCRIBE...

1 YOU'LL PAY ONLY £1 FOR THE FIRST FOUR ISSUES OF MATCH!

2 YOU'LL NEVER MISS AN ISSUE OF YOUR FAVOURITE MAG!

3 FREE UK DELIVERY TO YOUR DOOR EVERY SINGLE ISSUE!

THREE EASY WAYS TO SUBSCRIBE...

CALL
0844 84 888 72
QUOTE: AN14

ONLINE
www.greatmagazines.
co.uk/match

POST
MAGAZINE SUBSCRIPTIONS,
FREEPOST, ED03995,
MARKET HARBOROUGH,
LE16 9BR

did you know?

Check out these facts and stats about footy in 2013!

52 Bradford became the first fourth-tier club to play in a League Cup final for 51 years when they met Swansea at Wembley on February 24!

13m 13,644,136 fans went to live Premier League games in 2012-13!

BARCLAYS PREMIER LEAGUE

804m An incredible 804 million homes worldwide watched Premier League football on TV in 2012-13!

Chelsea became only the second English club in 29 years to win the Europa League when they beat Benfica back in May!

Jose Mourinho became Chelsea's 17th Premier League manager when he returned to Stamford Bridge for his second spell in charge back in June!

24 The 2013-14 season is Man. United and Wales ace Ryan Giggs' 24th in the top flight. What a star!

Cristiano Ronaldo and Lionel Messi scored a combined total of 130 goals for club and country in 2012-13!

128m Mega-rich Monaco spent £128 million in just two months to sign 11 new players in the summer of 2013!